17.84

010

Once There Was a
Tadpole

For Jeremy—J.A.

For Hannah, Carl, Heather,
and little miss trouble!—M.G.

First edition for the United States, its territories
and dependencies, and Canada published in 2010
by Barron's Educational Series, Inc.

First published in 2009 by Wayland
Copyright © Wayland 2009

Wayland
338 Euston Road
London, NW1 3BH

All inquiries should be addressed to:
Barron's Educational Series, Inc.
250 Wireless Boulevard
Hauppauge, NY 11788
www.barronseduc.com

The right of Judith Anderson to be identified as the author
of the work has been asserted by her in accordance with
the Copyright, Designs, and Patents Act 1988.

Editor: Nicole Edwards
Designer: Paul Cherrill
Digital Color: Carl Gordon

Library of Congress Control Number: 2009933531

ISBN-13: 978-0-7641-4496-7
ISBN-10: 0-7641-4496-0

Date of Manufacture: December 2009
Manufactured by: WKT, Shenzhen, China

Printed in China
9 8 7 6 5 4 3 2 1

Nature's Miracles

Once There Was a
Tadpole

Written by
Judith Anderson

Illustrated by
Mike Gordon

BARRON'S

Springtime is fun.
There are many new
things to look out for.
I look out for frogspawn.

Each egg has
a ball of jelly on
the outside, to
protect it.

The eggs stick
together.

If they didn't, they
wouldn't last very long!

My sister wants to
take a little bit of
frogspawn home.

8

But we don't take it from the river. We take it from our friend's backyard pond.

After a few days, we see a change. Each dot gets bigger and grows a little tail.

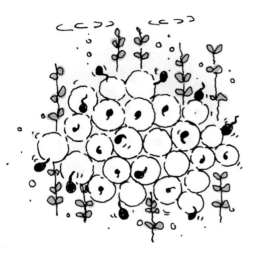

It wiggles its tail very hard, to push its way out of the jelly. It eats some of the jelly, too.

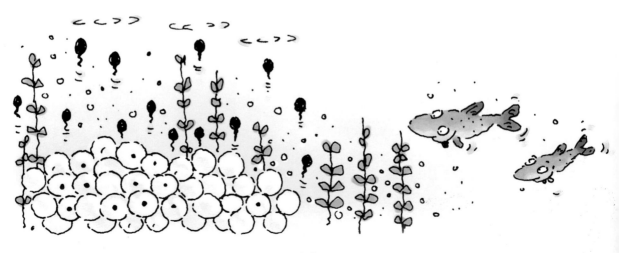

The dot has become a
tadpole! At first the tadpole
is just like a fish. It breathes
underwater through little slits
called gills.

But after two or three weeks, its gills disappear. Eventually, the tadpole must swim to the surface to breathe in air.

Just like we do.

Tadpoles need to eat in order to grow. They use their tiny lips and teeth to nibble on plants in the water.

They need plenty of food. They also need clean water, warmth, and shade.

When the tadpole's body is the size of a fat pea, two bumps appear on its sides. Soon these bumps grow into back legs.

Then two more bumps appear.
Guess what these will grow into?

Now the tadpole is changing quickly. First, its tail gets shorter. Its eyes start to bulge and its mouth gets wider.

It starts to eat insects
and little worms.

Twelve weeks after
hatching, the tadpole's
tail has vanished altogether.

It's time to put you back.

It looks like a little frog. Now it is called a froglet!

The froglet begins to climb
out of the water and spend
time on dry land.

After about three
years, it has finished
growing.

Now it is
an adult frog.

In the spring, the adult frog looks for a mate. He croaks to get the female's attention.

The female frog lays her eggs in a safe place in the water, and the male frog fertilizes them.

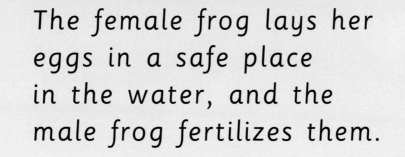

Next spring, we'll go looking
for frogspawn again. And the
frogspawn will hatch into tadpoles
again. And the tadpoles will change
into frogs again!

It's a life cycle—a life story that goes around and around, over and over again!

NOTES FOR PARENTS AND TEACHERS

Suggestions for reading the book with children

As you read this book with children, you may find it helpful to stop and discuss what is happening page by page. Children might like to talk about what the pictures show, and point out the changes taking place in the young tadpole and froglet. What other changes can they see?

The idea of a life cycle is developed throughout the book, and reinforced on the final pages. Ask the children if they know of any other life cycles. Can they see any patterns in nature? The other titles in the series may help them think about this.

Discussing the subject of tadpoles and frogs may introduce children to a number of unfamiliar words, including frogspawn, gills, mate, and fertilize. Make a list of new words and discuss what they mean.

Nature's Miracles

There are four titles about cycles in nature in the **Nature's Miracles** series: *Once There Was a Tadpole*; *Once There Was a Seed*; *Once There Was a Caterpillar*; and *Once There Was a Raindrop*. Each book encourages children to explore the natural world for themselves through direct observation and specific activities. The books emphasize developing a sense of responsibility toward plants, animals, and natural resources.

Once There Was a Tadpole will help young readers think about where and how tadpoles and

30

frogs live in the world around them. The book provides learning and discussion opportunities by introducing the idea that frogspawn, tadpoles, and frogs require specific conditions for survival and reproduction.

Suggestions for follow-up activities

The children in this book take a small amount of frogspawn home and place it in a suitable tank where they can watch the tadpoles develop. Rearing frogspawn at home or in school enables children to observe for themselves the process of change (or metamorphosis) that takes place and encourages a caring attitude toward wildlife. Only take frogspawn from a backyard pond, as this will be less invasive to the natural environment. The conditions in which you keep frogspawn need to be monitored carefully:

- Use fresh rainwater or water taken from the pond—not straight from the tap. If the water turns brown and murky, replace some of it with fresh pond water or rainwater.
- Provide some pond weed for young tadpoles to cling to, feed from, and shelter under. Remember that older tadpoles need more than weed to eat. Try a little fish food.
- Make sure the tank or pond is not in direct sunlight—some shade is best. Cover an open tank with netting to deter predators.
- Provide a flat rock so that froglets can crawl out of the water.
- Release them back into their original habitat before they are big enough to hop away.

A note on health and safety: Water presents many potential hazards for children. They should always be accompanied by a responsible adult when investigating ponds and streams.

Books to read

Why Should I Protect Nature? by Jen Green (Barron's, 2005)
Why Should I Save Water? by Jen Green (Barron's, 2005)
Let's Take Care of Our New Frog by Alejandro Algarra (Barron's, 2008)

Useful websites

www.42explore.com/frogs.htm

www.webtech.kennesaw.edu/jcheek3/frogs.htm

Index